History of the World

The American Revolution

Don Nardo

KidHaven Press

KidHaven Press, an imprint of Gale Group, Inc.
10911 Technology Place, San Diego, CA 92127

On Cover: Washington crossing the Delaware

Library of Congress Cataloging-in-Publication Data

Nardo, Don, 1947–
   The American Revolution / by Don Nardo.
      p. cm. — (History of the world)
   Includes bibliographical references and index.
   Summary: Provides a concise overview of the Revolutionary War,
   emphasizing the major battles and the military and political leaders
   of the Colonists and the British.
      ISBN 0-7377-0953-7 (hardback : alk. paper)
      1. United States—History—Revolution, 1775–1783—Juvenile
   literature. [1. United States—History—Revolution, 1775–1783.]
   I. Title.
      E208 .N25 2002
      973.3—dc21

2001002554

Printed in the U.S.A.

Contents

Chapter One

"The Shot Heard Round the World"

During the morning of April 19, 1775, about seven hundred British soldiers entered Lexington and Concord, at that time small villages in the British colony of Massachusetts. The soldiers found large groups of armed, angry colonists waiting for them. Shots rang out in both villages. Several men on both sides were killed or wounded before the British decided to withdraw.

These battles were neither large nor decisive. And if no other fighting had followed, history might have forgotten them. However, a great deal of fighting and loss of life did follow them. They turned out to be the opening battles of the American Revolution (also known as the Revolutionary War). This conflict, fought between 1775 and 1782, pitted Britain, the strongest country on Earth, against its American

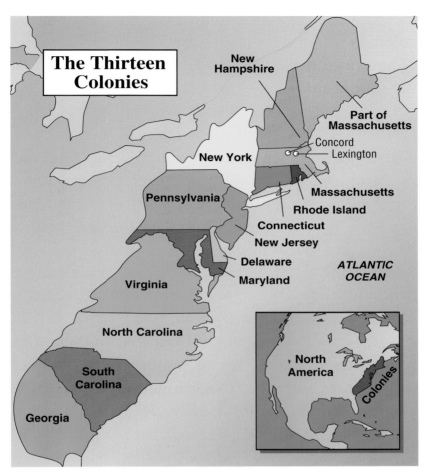

The Thirteen Colonies

New Hampshire

Part of Massachusetts

Concord
Lexington

New York

Massachusetts

Pennsylvania

Rhode Island

Connecticut

New Jersey

Delaware

ATLANTIC OCEAN

Virginia

Maryland

North Carolina

North America

South Carolina

Colonies

Georgia

colonies. After a desperate, bloody struggle, the colonists won. Their victory made it possible for them to break free of Britain and form a new country: the United States.

In time, the United States became a great nation. Its democratic ideas and government influenced countries in all corners of the globe. Therefore, the American Revolution signaled the birth not only of the United States but also of modern democracy. American poet Ralph Waldo Emerson captured this idea in words. On a monument erected to honor the colonists who fought and died at Concord, he wrote, "Here once the embattled farmers stood, and fired the shot heard round the world."[1]

Britain Taxes the Colonies

The anger that exploded at Lexington and Concord on that April day in 1775 had been building for a long time. In fact, the dramatic series of events leading up to that day began more than a decade before. In the early 1760s all American colonists were loyal British subjects. At the time, the idea of breaking free of the mother country was unthinkable. Americans were proud to be part of the British Empire. Britain was not only strong and rich, but it also granted its citizens many freedoms and rights that most other countries did not. The colonists enjoyed considerable freedom of speech and the press. Britain also allowed them to tax themselves when and how they saw fit. This seemed fair to all. And as long as Britain treated the colonies fairly, the colonists felt content with British rule.

Eventually, though, the colonists began to feel that the mother country was *not* treating them fairly. The first major complaint they had with Britain involved taxes. The British had recently been involved in a major conflict with France. Known as the French and Indian War, it had ended in 1763 with a British victory. British leaders wanted to keep their army large in case the French started another war.

Lexington, the site of the first battle of the Revolutionary War.

But equipping and paying so many troops was very expensive.

To raise the money it needed, **Parliament,** the British legislature, decided to tax the American colonies. In 1765 Parliament passed the Stamp Act, which forced the colonists to pay taxes on paper. This affected all sorts of items made from paper, such as legal and business documents, newspapers, pamphlets, playing cards, and so forth.

"No Taxation Without Representation"

American reaction to the Stamp Act was swift, loud, and violent. Colonists from all walks of life rose in protest. In New York an angry crowd broke into the royal governor's coach house and forced a British official to burn the paper stored there. Enraged citizens in Boston destroyed the homes of local tax collectors. And similar protests occurred on the streets of every colony.

Meanwhile, the local legislatures of the various colonies met to decide what to do about the new taxes. The Virginia legislature, known as the House of Burgesses, issued a public statement that read, in part, "The General Assembly of this colony has the sole right and power to lay taxes on the inhabitants of this colony." Allowing anyone outside the colony to tax Virginians would "destroy British as well as American freedom." [2] Furthermore, any non-Virginian trying to impose taxes on the colony would be viewed as an enemy of its people.

The thirteen colonies also issued a joint protest. **Delegates** from each colony met in October 1765 in what became known as the Stamp Act Congress. This was the first major expression of colonial unity. The delegates demanded that Parliament lift the stamp tax. They pointed out that the colonists had

Colonists burn British stamps to protest the Stamp Act.

no representatives in Parliament to support and defend their interests. It was therefore unfair for that body to impose its will on them. Cries of "No taxation without representation!" rose throughout America.

Both Sides Express Outrage

British leaders were surprised and disturbed by the angry colonial reaction to the Stamp Act. They feared they would not be able to enforce it without resorting to armed force. So they canceled, or **repealed** it in March 1766. When the news of the repeal reached America, celebrations erupted in every colony.

The happy mood did not last long, however. The British still needed money to support their troops. So, in 1767 they added a new tax on goods sent from Britain to the colonies. This meant that the colonists had to pay a good deal more for such important items as glass, lead, paint, and tea. Once again, the colonists were outraged. This time they not only protested but also **boycotted**, or refused to buy, British goods bearing the extra tax. British merchants lost a great deal of money. As a result, in 1770 Parliament repealed the tax on all goods except tea.

Many colonists continued to boycott British tea. A few, however, called for more drastic action. On December 16, 1773, a gang of men in Boston dressed up like Indians. They went to the local docks and dumped 342 chests of British tea into the harbor, an episode that became known as the

Bostonians cheer as colonists dressed as Indians dump British tea into the harbor.

Boston Tea Party. This time the British were the ones who expressed outrage. Responding to what Britain called willful destruction of property, Parliament passed the Coercive Acts in 1774. These laws closed the port of Boston until the colonists paid for the lost tea. They also forced colonists to let British troops live in their homes.

An Attack on One Is an Attack on All

The British thought they could make an example of Massachusetts and teach all of the colonies a lesson in obedience, but the plan backfired. Several Virginia patriots, including George Washington, Thomas Jefferson, and Patrick Henry, met and declared, "An attack made on one of our sister colonies is an attack made on all British America."[3]

Soon afterward, in September 1774, fifty-six delegates from twelve of the thirteen colonies met in Philadelphia. The meeting became known as the First Continental Congress. A few delegates, including Patrick Henry, called for a split with the mother country. Most, however, did not want to go that far. Therefore, the congress sent Parliament a formal complaint, demanding that the British "restore us to that state in which both countries found happiness and prosperity."[4]

Fearing the British would ignore the complaint, a number of colonists began stockpiling weapons. This concerned the British officials who oversaw the

Virginia's Patrick Henry addresses the members of the First Continental Congress.

colonies. In April 1775 the royal governor in Boston learned that local patriots had stored some arms in nearby Concord. So, during the night of April 18 he sent seven hundred troops to find and collect the weapons.

Early the next morning the British troops met about eighty armed colonists in Lexington. The British commander called on the men to throw down their guns. They refused, and both sides fired at each other. Leaving eight Americans dead and several wounded, the British marched on to Concord. In the next few hours, nearly 4,000 angry colonists gathered. Another, larger battled occurred. When it was over, the British counted 73 dead and 174 wounded. Colonial casualties were 50 killed and 34 wounded. America's War of Independence had begun.

Chapter  Two

A New Nation Faces an Uphill Fight

The bloodshed at Lexington and Concord proved to be the point of no return on the road to revolution and an independent America. American patriot and writer Thomas Paine put it this way:

> All plans, proposals, etc. prior to the 19th of April, i.e., to the **commencement** [opening] of **hostilities** [fighting], are like the almanacs of last year, which are useless now. The independence of America should have been considered as dating from *the first musket that was fired against her*.[5]

However, Paine, like Patrick Henry, was one of the more extreme patriots. Even after the loss of life

Thomas Paine wrote about the need for American independence.

at Lexington and Concord, many Americans did not want war. Nor did they want to form a new country separate from Britain. Among them were more moderate patriots, such as George Washington and Thomas Jefferson. They still hoped to settle the disputes with Britain peacefully. All they really wanted was to enjoy their full rights as Englishmen, which they felt British leaders had lately denied them.

But even these moderate patriots eventually joined the ranks of the **radicals.** In July 1775 John Jay and other moderates drafted the Olive Branch Petition. This document addressed the British king, George III. It requested that he consider the claim that Parliament had treated the colonies unfairly. The king, however, refused even to read the petition.

Making matters worse, in August of that year George III sent the colonists a message of his own. It declared them to be rebels who needed to be taught a lesson. Men like Jefferson, Washington, and Jay finally saw no other choice: They would have to fight and win independence from the mother country. They did not make this decision lightly, however. They knew that a war against Britian would be very hard to win.

The Declaration of Independence

Despite the odds against them, by early June 1776 most American leaders were committed to the cause of independence. These men held many private discussions. Then, on June 7, Virginian Richard Henry Lee offered a **resolution**, or proposal, to the Continental Congress. It read, in part, "Congress should

Thomas Jefferson reads his first draft of the Declaration of Independence to Benjamin Franklin.

declare that the United colonies are, and of right ought to be, free and independent states, that all political connection between them and Great Britain is, and ought to be, totally dissolved [broken]."[6]

The patriots considered Lee's idea, and then they decided to write a formal statement announcing American independence. On June 11 the Continental Congress asked a group of five men to carry out this task. The five were Thomas Jefferson, John Adams (of Massachusetts), Robert Livingston (of New York), Benjamin Franklin (of Pennsylvania), and Roger Sherman (of Connecticut). These men met privately and decided that Jefferson should write the first

Thomas Jefferson, Benjamin Franklin, John Adams, and the other founders revise the Declaration of Independence.

draft. One reason for this was that they all felt that he was the best writer in the group. Jefferson worked alone on the second floor of a house in Philadelphia from June 12 until June 28. Then he showed the finished draft to the others, who made a few small changes.

On July 1 the Continental Congress met to debate Lee's resolution, which was accepted the following day. That same day, it began debating Jefferson's draft for the declaration. For two days, the patriots argued about and made changes in the document. They completed the **revisions** on July 4. The finished product—the Declaration of Independence—is filled with stirring phrases about equality and freedom. Among the most famous are "All men are created equal." The key lines announcing American independence are, "We therefore, the Representatives of the United States of America, in General Congress . . . [do] solemnly publish and declare, That these United Colonies are, and of Right ought to be Free and Independent States."

The Problem of the Loyalists
In the days and weeks that followed, copies of the declaration were sent to people far and wide. And many Americans celebrated their independence from Britain. However, just as many of the former colonists did *not* celebrate. In fact, numerous people in every state had strong **misgivings** about separating from and fighting Britain.

One reason for such doubts and fears was that some Americans could not imagine not being British. They had been loyal British subjects all of their lives. Although they disagreed with some things that Britain had done recently, they did not want to part with the mother country. Because they were still loyal to Britain, they became known as "loyalists." Their numbers were larger than most people today realize. Of about 2.5 million people living in the new nation in 1776, John Adams estimated that about a third, or nearly 850,000, were loyal to the king. (Another

Angry patriots throw a local loyalist out of their town.

third, he said, were patriots like himself. The rest did not care who governed them.)

The presence of so many loyalists in the country made fighting a war against Britain very difficult. First, loyalists were everywhere—in all of the cities and scattered throughout the countryside. Many of them considered the patriots to be traitors. So, they often spied on their neighbors and reported what they saw and heard to the British. Moreover, almost fifty thousand loyalists fought on the British side against the patriots.

Military Advantages and Disadvantages

Many Americans, both loyalists and patriots, worried about or argued against fighting Britain for another reason. Simply put, they felt America had no chance of winning such a war. A respected New Yorker, Charles Inglis, wrote a popular pamphlet in 1776. It stated, "Devastation and ruin must mark the progress of this war. Our seacoasts and ports will be ruined, and our ships taken. Torrents [rivers] of blood will be spilled and thousands [of people] reduced to beggars."[7]

Inglis and those who agreed with him pointed out that the British army was large and well trained. In fact, during the war the British often had more than thirty thousand soldiers in action. By contrast, the American forces, known as the Continental army, were much smaller. At their largest, they consisted of twenty thousand regulars. These were soldiers who

American patriots fire on and drive back British red-coats at Concord Bridge.

signed up to serve for several months or years. More often, the commander of the army, George Washington, had as few as five thousand to ten thousand regulars.

The state militias sometimes helped the regulars. Militiamen were farmers and shopkeepers like those who fought at Lexington and Concord. When the enemy was near, they grabbed their weapons, fought a battle, and then returned to their farms and shops. Helpful though they were, they lacked the training and discipline of British regulars.

Britain's military strength was even greater on the seas. The British navy was the world's largest. When the American Revolution began Britain had twenty-eight large warships in American waters. These ships could keep supplies from reaching colonial ports. They could also ferry British troops quickly from one place to another. The Americans had only small sailboats and cargo ships. They built a few warships in 1776 and 1777, but the enemy burned or captured most of them by 1779.

In short, as the war began America was a divided country with many citizens having no heart for the fight. And the British clearly had the military upper hand. In April 1776 John Adams grimly predicted, "We shall have a long, obstinate [stubborn], and bloody war to go through."[8] He turned out to be right.

Chapter Three

A Countryside in Arms

Britain's military might became clear in the first major battle fought after the colonies declared their independence in July 1776. In that month a British general, William Howe, moved on New York City. At the time, it was America's second-largest city (after Philadelphia). Howe reasoned that gaining control of New York would give him an important stronghold. From there, he could strike at nearby cities and states more easily. Also, he hoped to cut off the New England states from the southern states. That would make it more difficult for the Americans to unify their forces.

George Washington tried to stop Howe. But in a large battle fought on Long Island on August 27, the Continental army suffered heavy losses. Washington had to withdraw his remaining men from the area. Soon afterward, Howe took possession of New York City.

American forces retreat after their defeat on Long Island in August 1776.

These losses brought America's military weaknesses into sharp focus. In addition to being much smaller than Britain's army, the Continental army had few trained officers. To his dismay, Washington had a hard time finding men with experience in commanding troops. Also, many of those who did have the needed experience were loyalists or had no interest in serving.

Experienced, trained soldiers were also in short supply. Part of the problem was that at first they served for a year or less. Not long after they received their training, their terms ended and they returned to civilian life. The troops who took their places had to be trained from scratch. "Good God!" Washington roared at some congressmen who visited him at his military camp. "Our cause is ruined if you engage men for only a year. If we ever hope for success, we must have men enlisted for the whole term of the war!"[9] Fortunately congress listened to Washington and increased term of service to three years.

Despite its weaknesses, the colonies did have one important advantage from the beginning of the conflict. Almost every time British troops marched inland from the sea, hundreds and sometimes thousands of militiamen and other locals rose up to fight them. Having to face a whole countryside of angry, armed

American militiamen rose to fight the British every time they marched inland.

people was new to the British. Back in Europe, an army could expect to march safely through the countryside until it met up with enemy troops. The local townspeople and peasants usually laid low or ran away. Seeing a countryside in arms made the British nervous, even fearful. So, for most of the war they avoided venturing too far inland, preferring to stay near the coast. There, the closeness of their ships and supply lines made them feel safer. This limitation worked in the Americans' favor.

Washington Crosses the Delaware

Another American advantage was the overconfidence of some British commanders. After General Howe took New York, for example, he was in a strong position while Washington was in a weak one. In addition to his recent losses on Long Island, Washington had to split up his remaining men. It was the only way to defend the large expanse of land lying west of New York. Howe should have immediately pursued and destroyed Washington's small, inexperienced forces when he had the chance.

But Howe ordered no pursuit. Winter was setting in, and he did not fancy the idea of fighting in the cold. Anyway, he was confident he could defeat the enemy any time he wanted. After all, Howe viewed Washington's army as nothing more than a pitiful group of rowdy farmers and troublemakers. Surely such men were no match for the mighty British army.

Therefore, Howe decided to winter his army in New York and nearby New Jersey. About half of Howe's troops in New Jersey were hired troops from Germany. The Germans looted American houses and shops, stealing everything in sight. Even worse, a large force of Germans occupied the town of Trenton, located on the Delaware River. This put them in striking distance of Philadelphia, then the colonial capital.

Not surprisingly, Washington was worried. Ever since the disaster on Long Island, things had gone from bad to worse for the Americans. On December 18 he wrote to his brother, "No man, I believe, ever had a greater choice of difficulties, and less means to [find a way out of] them."[10] The next day Thomas Paine wrote, "These are the times that try men's souls. Tyranny, like hell, is not easily conquered."[11] Moreover, he said, the harder the struggle the Americans had to endure, the more glorious their final victory would be.

Washington felt he had to score such a victory, and soon, or the American cause might be lost. So he hatched a daring plan. On Christmas Day 1776 he led twenty-four hundred soliders across the Delaware during the middle of the night. The next morning they completely surprised the Germans at Trenton. The entire force of almost a thousand men surrendered.

An Invasion from the North
As the news of the victory at Trenton spread, American patriots everywhere took heart. Pennsylvania

Washington leads his army across the Delaware River on Christmas Day in 1776.

militiamen poured into Washington's camp to aid the exhausted regulars. On January 2, 1777, barely a week after Trenton, the Americans won another battle. Washington seized Princeton, New Jersey, from the British. Later that winter, he drove the enemy out of several other New Jersey towns.

Later in 1777 the Americans scored still another important victory. Britain's General John Burgoyne led an army southward from Canada by way of Lake Champlain (on the border between New York and Vermont). Hundreds of Mohawk Indians reinforced the British units. The goal was to invade and conquer northern New York and the New England states.

But Burgoyne soon encountered the awesome power of a countryside in arms. Seemingly out of nowhere, groups of local patriots attacked and defeated his units. "Wherever the King's forces point," he complained, "militia to the number of three or four thousand assemble in a few hours."[12] Burgoyne lost so many men (through death, wounding, or desertion) that he finally could not go on. On October 17 he surrendered to American general Horatio Gates.

Britain Had Only Begun to Fight

Burgoyne's defeat gave another boost to American morale. Some Americans who had earlier seen challenging Britain as foolish and hopeless changed their minds. However, most British generals were not wor-

Britain's General John Burgoyne surrenders to America's General Horatio Gates at Saratoga, New York.

ried. They, like George Washington and his own generals, knew that Britain had only begun to fight. So far, the British had committed only a small fraction of their forces to the war in America. They could and would send more. Furthermore, Britain still controlled the coastal waters. As long as it did so, the Americans could not win the war.

Then, an event in faraway Europe changed everything. In February 1778 America signed a treaty of alliance with France. That country had armies and navies equal to those of Britain. Suddenly, the British generals had good reason to worry.

Chapter  Four

"The World Turned Upside Down"

American leaders were not surprised by the news that France had entered the war on their side. They had been asking France for help for over two years. Late in 1775, well before the Declaration of Independence, Congress had sent secret messages to the French government. These were mainly requests to buy arms.

Then in October 1776, Congress sent Benjamin Franklin to France. To his delight, he found that the French loved the Americans. And they heartily approved of the American Revolution. French leaders, still upset about losing an earlier war to Britain, welcomed it as a way to weaken Britain and its empire. French merchants saw America as a rich new trade market. And French thinkers were impressed and inspired by American ideals of freedom and

Benjamin Franklin receives a warm welcome at the court of France's King Louis XVI.

human rights. As a result, Franklin found himself the darling of French society.

Still, French leaders were slow to recognize American independence and forge a French-American alliance. Doing so would plunge France into another war with Britain. The French told Franklin that they first needed to see some sign that the Americans had a chance of winning. That sign finally came when Britain's General Burgoyne surrendered in New York late in 1777. On February 6, 1778, Franklin and French officials signed an agreement. They pledged to fight together until Britain recognized American independence.

Brutality in the Carolinas

American patriots rejoiced at the news of the pact with France, but their joy soon began to fade. The French proved to be very slow in mounting an attack. They finally sent a fleet of warships commanded by Count D'Estaing in 1779. However, after suffering heavy losses in a battle near Tybee Island in Georgia, D'Estaing sailed his ships back to France.

French leaders assured Congress that they would send more ships and troops. In the meantime, though, it was clear that the Americans would be on their own for a while. During the next year and a half, the war continued to be a **stalemate.** Because he lacked sea power, Washington could not force the British out of New York and other coastal strongholds. And the British dared not venture too far inland. They still feared masses of country folk rising against them.

Most of the fighting in this period took place in North and South Carolina. It proved to be the bloodiest and most tragic combat of the war. Both sides resorted to attacking civilians and destroying property. The British captured Charleston, South Carolina, one of the most important American ports, in May 1780. The general in charge, Lord Charles Cornwallis, then launched a brutal assault on nearby villages and farms. One local farmer wrote to his cousin that the British robbed him of his "horses, cows, sheep, clothing, [and] money until we were stripped naked."[13] This man was lucky to escape with his life. Bands of British redcoats murdered or tortured many other civilians.

Americans desperately defend their position against attacking British in the Carolinas.

At the same time, rebel bands launched similar cruel attacks on loyalists who were helping the British. The Carolina countryside erupted in revenge raids as neighbor fought neighbor; sometimes whole families were killed and their homes burned. Meanwhile, gangs of outlaws, often disguised as soldiers, attacked both loyalists and patriots. A local minister wrote, "[Society] seems to be at an end. Robberies and murders are often committed on the public roads. Poverty and hardship [are] everywhere, and the morals of the people are almost entirely [gone]." [14]

Nathaniel Greene Enters the Fight

Eventually the bloody stalemate in the Carolinas ended in the Americans' favor. Late in 1780 Congress sent a very capable general to take charge of patriot forces in the south. His name was Nathaniel Greene. The army he received consisted of only about a thousand regulars and five hundred militiamen. And they were in sad shape. Greene later wrote, "The appearance of the troops was wretched [awful] beyond description." [15] Many lacked food and wore torn clothes. And their mood was gloomy.

But Greene succeeded in whipping his soldiers into shape. And on January 17, 1781, he led them to victory over the British at Cowpens (near the border between the two Carolinas). In the months that followed, Greene continued to hammer the British. He lost some battles, but even as he did he inflicted heavy losses on the enemy. Finally, he drove the British back to Charleston.

Cornwallis now realized that he could not defeat the Americans in the Carolinas. He decided to try to

Nathaniel Greene, who defeated the British at Cowpens in January 1781.

win the war in Virginia instead. In April 1781 he headed north. He soon set up headquarters at Yorktown, facing Chesapeake Bay in southern Virginia. He had no way of knowing that this move would prove his undoing.

The Old Order Crumbles

At the very moment Cornwallis was getting settled in Yorktown, a new French fleet was speeding toward Virginia. It consisted of twenty huge warships under the command of Count de Grasse. When Washington learned that the fleet was on its way, he could barely contain his joy. One witness said he "acted like a child whose every wish has been gratified [fulfilled]."[16] Meanwhile, almost seven thousand French regulars had already landed in Rhode Island. They joined Washington's small army.

These allied forces, along with over three thousand Virginia militiamen, swiftly converged on Yorktown. The shocked Cornwallis soon found himself trapped. The American and French troops surrounded him on his land side. And de Grasse's ships blocked any attempt to escape by sea. On September 28, 1781, the allies opened fire on Yorktown from both sides. It did not take long for Cornwallis to realize his position was hopeless; he surrendered his entire army on October 19. Everyone present, including Cornwallis, knew that after this major defeat the British would no longer have the stomach to go on. The war was over. The new country had won its freedom from Britain.

General Charles Cornwallis (left) surrenders to General George Washington at Yorktown.

The news of the great victory passed quickly from town to town and state to state. Americans of all walks of life poured into the streets and embraced one another. Some cried for joy. Meanwhile, the British troops at Yorktown laid down their guns and marched grimly out of the town. They walked between two lines of soldiers, one American, the other French. As they did so, a military band played a tune titled "The World Turned Upside Down."

This choice of music turned out to be strangely fitting. In a way, the successful birth of the United States did mark a new beginning for the world. In the years that followed, people in many nations followed

After the war ends, Washington receives a hero's welcome in New York City.

the Americans' example and launched revolutions to attain freedom. As a result, the old European order of kings and empires steadily began to crumble. In this way, the American Revolution did more than create a new country. "The shot heard round the world" changed that world forever.

Notes

Chapter One: "The Shot Heard Round the World"

1. Ralph Waldo Emerson, "Concord Hymn," in *Favorite Poems Old and New*, ed. Helen Ferris. Garden City, NY: Doubleday, 1957, p. 422.
2. Quoted in Max Beloff, ed., *The Debate on the American Revolution, 1761–1783*. London: Adam and Charles Black, 1960, p. 71.
3. Quoted in Henry S. Commager and Richard B. Morris, eds., *The Spirit of Seventy-Six: The Story of the American Revolution as Told by Participants*, vol. 1. New York: Bobbs-Merrill, 1958, p. 39.
4. Quoted in Samuel E. Morison, ed., *Sources and Documents Illustrating the American Revolution, 1764–1788, and the Formation of the Federal Constitution*. Oxford, England: Clarendon Press, 1953, pp. 119, 122.

Chapter Two: A New Nation Faces an Uphill Fight

5. Thomas Paine, *Common Sense*, in *John Dos Passos Presents the Living Thoughts of Thomas Paine*. New York: Fawcett, 1963, pp. 60, 78.
6. Quoted in Adrienne Koch and William Peden, eds., *The Life and Selected Writings of Thomas Jefferson*. New York: Random House, 1944, p. 14.

7. Quoted in William Dudley, ed., *The American Revolution: Opposing Viewpoints.* San Diego: Greenhaven, 1992, pp. 154–55.

8. Quoted in Samuel E. Morison, *The Oxford History of the American People.* New York: Oxford University Press, 1965, p. 224.

Chapter Three: A Countryside in Arms

9. Quoted in Morison, *Oxford History of the American People,* p. 225.

10. Quoted in Morison, *Oxford History of the American People,* p. 243.

11. Thomas Paine, *Crisis,* quoted in Dudley, *The American Revolution,* p. 182.

12. Quoted in Morison, *Oxford History of the American People,* p. 248.

Chapter Four: "The World Turned Upside Down"

13. Quoted in James W. Davidson et al., *Nation of Nations: A Narrative History of the American Republic.* New York: McGraw-Hill, 1990, p. 218.

14. Quoted in Davidson et al., *Nation of Nations,* p. 218.

15. Quoted in Morison, *Oxford History of the American People,* p. 259.

16. Quoted in Morison, *Oxford History of the American People,* p. 263.

Glossary

boycott: To refuse to buy certain goods in an effort to punish the seller.

commencement: An opening or beginning.

delegate: A person representing a town, state, or other group at a joint meeting.

hostilities: Fighting.

misgivings: Doubts.

Parliament: Britain's legislature, similar in some ways to the U.S. Congress.

radical: Drastic or revolutionary.

repeal: To cancel or eliminate.

resolution: A proposal, usually in a meeting or legislature.

revisions: Changes.

stalemate: A draw, or a situation in which neither of two opposing sides can achieve any advantage.

For Further Exploration

Margaret Cousins, *Ben Franklin of Old Philadelphia*. New York: Random House, 1980. The main events and characters of the years leading up to the American Revolution are captured in this biography of one of the principal U.S. founding fathers. Aimed at junior high school readers.

Richard Ferrie, *The World Turned Upside Down: George Washington and the Battle of Yorktown*. New York: Holiday House Books, 1999. A lavishly illustrated and very well-written description of the victory that decided the Revolutionary War. Highly recommended for young readers.

Stuart A. Kallen, *The Declaration of Independence*. Edina, MN: Abdo and Daughters, 1994; and R. Conrad Stein, *The Declaration of Independence*. Chicago: Childrens Press, 1995. These two recent, nicely illustrated volumes present the basic facts about the Declaration of Independence for grade school readers.

Don Nardo, *Opposing Viewpoints Digests: The Revolutionary War*. San Diego: Greenhaven, 1998. Provides a collection of essays containing a wide range of opinions and debates by American colonists about whether it was a good idea to go to war with the British.

Walter Oleksy, *The Boston Tea Party*. New York: Franklin Watts, 1993. The events and personalities shaping this famous incident leading up to the American Revolution are told here in a simple format for basic readers.

Dian Silox-Jarrett, *Heroines of the American Revolution: America's Founding Mothers*. Chapel Hill, NC: Green Angel, 1998. This book has a lot of interesting information for young readers about some of the women who played important parts in the Revolutionary War. Be aware that some of the dialogue is fictional.

Brian Williams, *George Washington*. New York: Marshall Cavendish, 1988. The story of the gentleman farmer who led the American army to victory in the Revolutionary War.

Index

Picture Credits

About the Author

Historian and award-winning author Don Nardo has written many books for young people about American history, including *The Mexican-American War*, *The Declaration of Independence*, *The U.S. Presidency*, and *Franklin D. Roosevelt: U.S. President*. Mr. Nardo lives with his wife, Christine, in Massachusetts.